The Almost Last Christmas

Tony McCaffrey & Dave Goulet

Illustrated by Paul Ritz Magtrayo

Paper back ISBN-13: 978-1-963272-12-3
Hardcover ISBN-13: 978-1-963272-15-4
Dyslexic Friendly ISBN-13: 978-1-963272-18-5

ShelteringTree.Earth, LLC Publishing
PO Box 973, Eagle Lake, FL 33839

Did you enjoy this book?

We love to hear from our readers.

Please visit the author and illustrator at
ShelteringTreeMedia.com

DEDICATION

To the children.

We wish we could leave you a better world. Our hope lives in you and our hope grows as you grow.

And a little child shall lead them (Isaiah 11:6 NKJV)[1]

[1] Scripture taken from the New King James Version®.

1 THE TRAINING ROOM

The film room became dark as all the new elves grew quiet so they could watch. These young elves were reaching the age when they would decide where they would work. Would they work beneath the North Pole? Or would they work on the space station hidden in the asteroid belt?

The elves were from another planet and their race was called the Gift Givers.

The film began. Santa appeared on the screen and began to talk.

"Everyone knows that I have a *Nice List* and a *Naughty List* for all the children on Earth. But did you know that all the planets in the Milky Way Galaxy are also on a *Nice List* or a *Naughty List*? The planets on the *Nice List* have people there that are very nice. Those planets have received great gifts from us Gift Givers."

All the elves in the film room yelled and clapped in delight. They would soon become Gift Givers when they figured out their future jobs.

Santa said more, "The planets on the *Nice List* receive new ways to clean up their planets and new sources of energy. Which list do you think the planet Earth is on?"

The elves looked down because they all knew the answer to that question.

Santa went on. "Well, I'm sorry to say that Earth is on the *Naughty List*. I have tried very hard to show humans how to be nice. But I have been here 250 years and humans still are not nice enough.

They are still greedy and often fight. They also need these gifts to clean up their planet. But these gifts are unsafe if not used by nice people. It only takes twenty or thirty years for most planets to get on the *Nice List.* Not Earth. The Gift Givers have been working hard to help humans get Earth on the *Nice List*. One day, it will happen and that will be a happy day indeed!"

The elves clapped and cheered. They looked forward to that day very much.

"By the way, humans call the Gift Givers by the name *elves* because they remind humans of fairy elves in the old folktales of Earth. The Gift Givers took on the name *elf,* but some made the letters stand for *Earth-like life form*. Others made the letters stand for *extraterrestrial life form*. Either way, it meant that the Gift Givers were from another planet."

The Gift Givers laughed loudly at how they changed the meaning of the word e*lf.*

The film next showed Santa on Christmas Eve from a few years ago. Santa has high-tech tools that he uses on Christmas Eve.

Santa does not have to visit every single house on Christmas Eve. Santa beams the presents into each home like you would see on the show *Star Trek.* One minute, there were no presents under the Christmas tree. The next minute, the presents are there. An energy beam delivers the presents.

There were "Ooohs" and "Aaahs" from the elves in the room. They liked the high-tech tools.

Also, Santa knows what every child wants for Christmas. But Santa doesn't really need to know. Santa uses quantum mechanics. What is inside a present is really every gift at the same time. What is inside is in a quantum state. Then, when a child opens the present and sees what is inside, it becomes what the child wants.

Further, those big humps in the back of Santa's sleigh? They are not bags of presents. They are satellite dishes that beam the presents into people's homes.

Santa stops his sleigh over a town or city, like Boston, for example. The beams come out from under the North Pole. They then bounce off the round dishes and down into homes. Santa then moves his sleigh above another town or city. The same thing happens again and again all night long until Christmas morning.

Finally, the reindeer are not really needed. They are just for show. They hide the high-tech that makes Santa's sleigh fly. The reindeer wear special horseshoes to make them fly.

The lights came up in the film room. Sitting in the middle of the front row was an elf that was a couple years older than the others. She was just visiting the space station where they trained the younger elves. Her name was EekaYor and she now worked with all the high-tech tools under the North Pole. She enjoyed watching the Santa films, so she watched them every time she visited the space station.

EekaYor was young but she was now on the High Council. She was the youngest elf in the group that made all the big decisions about Earth. She wore a green vest and skirt, with candy-cane striped sleeves and leggings. Her red hair matched the red on the sleeves and leggings.

2 INTRODUCING EEKAYOR

EekaYor stood up and turned to wave at many of the younger elves. EekaYor was their hero. In just a couple of years she had worked her way up to be on the High Council. She left the film room out of the side door. She walked down the long hall to the huge room where the High Council met to make the big decisions about Earth.

She entered the big room. It was made out of white stone. It had very high ceilings. All the chairs and the big table were also made out of white stone. EekaYor walked to the far end of the long table. The other members of the High Council were already seated along the sides of the table. Each one wore an elf's hat that had its own bright pattern of colors. Each nodded at EekaYor as she passed by. The elves around the table each had beards and were so much older than EekaYor was. The other elves around the table were quiet because they were afraid of the leader of the High Council. They always did what the leader wanted to do. EekaYor was also afraid of him.

The head of the High Council then walked into the big room. Everyone froze out of fear. He was taller than the other elves. His elf hat was taller, and his clothes were not bright and colorful. They were dark and grey. He had a loud voice, and he was not afraid to use it. His name was KisQualley. He sat down at the near end of the table.

"Today is December 19. We shall discuss whether Earth should be given more time to get on the *Nice List,*" KisQualley began. "They have been given 250 years. Most planets only take about thirty years. They will never get off the *Naughty List*. I think we should give up on Earth after this upcoming Christmas."

Even though EekaYor was afraid of KisQualley, she liked humans. She thought that Earth could get on the *Nice List* someday. She stood up and her legs shook a bit from being scared. She grasped a picture in her pocket of her human friend. It was a little girl. That helped EekaYor feel braver. She spoke up loud and clear.

"Earth needs our help so much," EekaYor began. "They need our help more than any other planet has needed us."

KisQualley spoke up loudly, "We give them the help of Santa. He shows them how to be nice. This is the way it has always been done. If Santa is not enough for them to get on the *Nice List*, then that is their problem."

"Earth needs extra help," EekaYor began again. "Why do we have to do things the same way with every single planet?"

"Because that is the way it has always been done," KisQualley spoke loudly and banged his fist on the stone table. "Your time is up, EekaYor, and Earth's time is up."

"No, it is not!" EekaYor spoke up. Her hands were now shaking. She was surprised that any words were coming out of her mouth.

"It is over!" KisQualley yelled. "EekaYor, you get out of this room, and we will have our vote." KisQualley's large hand pointed straight at the door.

EekaYor tried to speak up once again, but she was shouted down by KisQualley. She left with her head down and went to the dock area where all the spaceships were kept.

3 FACING MR. HANCOCK

The big room with white stones was inside a space station, which was inside a very large asteroid in the asteroid belt. The Gift Givers made the asteroid hollow. They beamed the stone on the inside of the asteroid to the outside of the asteroid. Then, they could build inside the hollow asteroid. It was a great hiding place for all their buildings and ships.

EekaYor hopped into her little starship called the *Yule*. She was very angry. She headed straight back to Earth. But, in order to hide her ship during the trip to Earth, her small ship was beamed inside a small hollow asteroid. Once inside, the small asteroid started heading toward Earth. From the outside, it just looked like a small rock headed to Earth. It was the perfect hiding place.

When EekaYor was close to Earth, her ship beamed out of the asteroid. She landed in the woods outside of New York City rather than the North Pole. EekaYor had an idea and needed to visit someone in New York. The asteroid missed the Earth and whizzed by it. It was daytime on December 20.

EekaYor landed near New York City. A plan was beginning to form in her mind for how to help Earth. EekaYor could not just give up on the Earth. She could not let the Gift Givers just leave Earth forever. She had to do more to get Earth on the *Nice List*.

EekaYor knew that KisQualley was good friends with a very rich human named Mr. Hancock. Gift Givers were not supposed to be friends with humans. But everyone knew that KisQualley and Mr. Hancock were friends. Maybe Mr. Hancock could change

KisQualley's mind. Maybe KisQualley would help Earth more if his friend asked him to. It was worth a try.

Mr. Hancock's office was in New York City. He was the biggest maker of toys in the world. Mr. Hancock was also the richest person on Earth.

EekaYor got out of her ship in the woods and made her way into the city. She wore a thick winter coat and the hood hid her pointy ears. A scarf hid most of her face.

She made her way into the downtown area with all those tall buildings and found her way to the building called the Hancock Building.

Before entering the building, EekaYor used another high-tech tool she had. She used a cloaking tool, which made it so no one can see you. This tool bent the light around you so that it looked like you were not there.

Using this tool, she easily snuck past the security officers on the main floor. She waited by the elevator until someone else opened the door and got onboard the elevator. Then, she snuck in the elevator and stood in a corner.

When the other person got off the elevator, EekaYor stayed on the elevator and hit the button for the top floor. The elevator door opened, and Mr. Hancock's assistant did not see anyone on the elevator. This had happened before, so the assistant looked down to her desk to carry on with her work. EekaYor quietly moved past the assistant's desk and moved to Mr. Hancock's office door. She opened the door, slipped inside, knocked on the inside of the door, and uncloaked so that Mr. Hancock could see her. The room was massive with bookshelves behind Mr. Hancock that went from the floor all the way up to the two-story ceiling. Beautiful plants and colorful flowers hung from the ceiling and the ceiling was made entirely of mirrors so you could see the plants by their reflection in the ceiling. Expensive paintings filled the walls on the left. The wall on the right was entirely made of glass and looked out over the city.

Mr. Hancock looked up from his large, wooden desk. He looked angry and annoyed. "What are you doing here?" he said. "I only speak with your leader."

EekaYor began, "When did you last speak with KisQualley?"

"About an hour ago," Mr. Hancock responded.

"You must know then that the Earth has just a few more days to get on the *Nice List*," EekaYor said.

"Maybe I do. Maybe I don't," Mr. Hancock replied. "What does it matter?"

EekaYor did not trust Mr. Hancock now. Any other human would have been upset about the Earth. But he did not seem to care.

EekaYor moved a bit closer to his desk and took something small out of her pocket. It was a tiny computer made out of cells, so it was alive. It was a bio-computer, and it was so small that it could not be seen. It was her latest invention. She touched Mr. Hancock's desk and this tiniest of computers began to move towards Mr. Hancock's computer. It crawled inside. It would get data from Mr. Hancock's computer and send it back to her.

"Come with me," Mr. Hancock said to EekaYor. "I want to show you my new idea for the future of the Earth after you aliens leave us on the *Naughty List*."

EekaYor's curiosity got the best of her and she followed him to another room. He opened the door for her and she walked into the room first. *BAM!* He slammed the door shut and locked it.

Mr. Hancock left. EekaYor yelled and banged on the door again and again. After a while, she got tired of yelling. So, she sat down on the floor next to the wall. She had her head down. This room was her prison.

After a while, EekaYor lifted up her head. She saw that this room had a high ceiling. It was maybe six or seven stories high. There was a window at the top called a skylight. All of a sudden, EekaYor knew how to get out.

How was she going to get out? The walls were smooth, so she could not climb them. Well, the Gift Givers are full of surprises. Mr. Hancock must not have known about this surprise or he would not have put her in this room.

The Gift Givers understood gravity very well. Their bodies responded to gravity in a different way than humans did. The bodies of humans were pushed down by gravity toward the Earth. The bodies of Gift Givers easily floated.

As children, they floated all the time. They had to learn not to float. They learned to focus their minds so they could stay on the ground. It was funny when they were asleep. They would just float around because their minds were relaxed. Some Gift Givers would tie one end of a rope to their ankle and the other end to a table leg. In this way, they would not float away.

In the locked room, EekaYor relaxed her mind a bit and she began to float. She slowly floated up to the top near the skylight. She broke the glass of the skylight with her shoe and floated out of the building and back to where her ship was.

4 INTRODUCING MACKACK

When EekaYor arrived back at her ship, the bio-computer had already sent her some interesting data from Mr. Hancock's computer.

"Oh, my goodness," EekaYor gasped.

Mr. Hancock was a trillionaire, but not from just selling toys. He also made a lot of money from secretly selling guns, tanks, jets, and rockets to both sides of any war. People thought he just sold toys. Mr. Hancock did not want humans to be on the *Nice List* because he made a lot of money when they were not nice.

"KisQualley must not know that Mr. Hancock is a bad guy," EekaYor thought. "But KisQualley needs to know this." KisQualley and EekaYor were not getting along right now. But she felt that she had to tell KisQualley about Mr. Hancock.

EekaYor took off in her little ship, the *Yule*, and headed back to the space station inside the asteroid. It was the morning of December 21.

After a long trip, she got back to where there were many asteroids, which is called the asteroid belt. She let the computer steer her ship. The ship turned this way and that way to avoid the big space rocks that were in her way. EekaYor remembered back to when she was young. She would fly her tiny ship at high speed and dodge all the asteroids. It was so much fun! She also had races with her friends in their tiny ships.

EekaYor did not race around the asteroids now. She was older and she let her computer do the work. She had so many important things to think about. Would the Gift Givers soon leave Earth? It looked like Earth was never going to get on the *Nice List* and meet the aliens. If Earth stayed on the *Naughty List*, then Earth would never receive the technology that could help it so much. Mr. Hancock was actually a human who wanted Earth to stay on the *Naughty List*. EekaYor could barely believe such a human could exist. EekaYor was worrying about many important things.

EekaYor looked at a picture that she had near the control panel on her ship. It was a picture of a young human girl named Tasha. EekaYor touched the picture gently. She remembered back to when she first met Tasha. Tasha was sleeping beneath her Christmas tree and EekaYor was on the Quality Inspection team checking out random houses to make sure that the presents beamed in at the proper location. Tasha caught EekaYor in her home and the two became friends. Even though aliens were not supposed to befriend humans, EekaYor broke this rule and visited Tasha at least twice a year.

If EekaYor had to leave Earth, she would never see Tasha again. EekaYor was sad but more determined than ever to get Earth on the *Nice List* so she could stay close to her best friend.

EekaYor landed her ship inside the asteroid with the space station. She walked through the shipping dock past all the other ships. She headed back to the big room where KisQualley yelled at her on her last visit. This big room was also where KisQualley had his office. He liked to be in this huge room all by himself. EekaYor made her way into the room and walked right up to KisQualley's big, stone desk. EekaYor thought that KisQualley would yell at her as soon as he saw her. But he did not yell. EekaYor told him that she had talked to Mr. Hancock on Earth. She told him that Mr. Hancock locked her up.

EekaYor thought she saw a little bit of anger on his face. He put his hand under his desk.

EekaYor knew what he was doing. She had seen him do this before. He was going to press the alarm button to call the guards. EekaYor took off running out of the room.

She ran away before the guards got to the big room. EekaYor did not know what she had done wrong. EekaYor ran back to the shipping dock. She knew that there would be guards at her ship waiting for her. So, she took a right turn, then a left turn, and ran in the other direction. She saw a ship that was open. She dove inside and hid behind all the cargo.

EekaYor heard the guards running nearby. A guard came into the open ship and looked around. EekaYor ducked her head way down behind the goods on the ship. Soon, the guard left and was gone.

The next thing that EekaYor heard was, "I know you're back there."

"Oh, no," EekaYor thought. "Somebody heard me."

She stayed in her hiding place for a while.

"It's OK," the voice said. "I won't turn you over to the guards."

EekaYor peaked up from her hiding place. She saw an elf with a huge red beard. She knew who he was. Everyone knew who he was. He was named MacKack and he took care of all the computers at the North Pole.

EekaYor was fairly new to the North Pole. She had run into MacKack a few times but did not really know him well. MacKack invented all the high-tech tools that Santa used on Christmas Eve. He invented how presents beamed into people's homes. He invented how presents became what people wanted them to be as soon as they looked at them.

"I will help you out," MacKack said. "I don't know your story right now, but I know you're on the computer team with me. So, I'm going to help you out."

MacKack's ship was now loaded up with all the tools that he needed. He got his ship out of there quickly. When it was safe, EekaYor came out of her hiding place and sat next to him as he flew the ship.

MacKack told EekaYor a silly joke, "What do you get when you beam the inside of an asteroid to the outside?"

"A smaller asteroid," EekaYor replied. They both laughed. It was a goofy, geeky joke. It calmed down EekaYor, who was quite nervous from being chased. They flew back to Earth together and on the way she told her story to him. He listened intently and they began to become friends.

MacKack and EekaYor had a long trip back to Earth. They had a lot of time to get to know each other. MacKack told her some of the stories of his inventions that helped Santa so much.

There was one invention MacKack had made that had never been tested before. He created the alarm system that would go off when Earth was ready to be on the *Nice List*. This alarm used the internet and social media. The alarm was set to go off when the internet was filled with joyful posts for a long time.

EekaYor was so happy hearing all of MacKack's stories about his inventions.

"I am an inventor, too," she told MacKack. "I invented a bio-computer that is too small to be seen with your eyes. It is alive and stores data in its DNA. One of them crawled into Mr. Hancock's computer."

"Wonderful," MacKack replied. "I can't wait to see what you invent next."

In talking further, EekaYor and MacKack agreed that KisQualley was not acting right. They also agreed that Mr. Hancock did not want Earth to get on the *Nice List*. They did not yet know if KisQualley and Mr. Hancock were working together to keep Earth off the *Nice List*. They started to plan a way to find out more about the relationship between KisQualley and Mr. Hancock.

EekaYor and MacKack knew that they could not return to the North Pole. By now, KisQualley had certainly told everyone at the North Pole to watch out for EekaYor. And most likely,

KisQualley would have figured out that MacKack was with EekaYor.

They had to go somewhere else. Where should they go? It was now the late afternoon on December 22.

As they got close to Earth, EekaYor had an idea. She instructed MacKack to fly his ship to a little town called North Hope, which had many forests around it. They could hide their ship there. He trusted her, so he set down the ship where she said.

"Follow me," EekaYor said. They got out of the ship and began to walk through the forest. When they got in a clear place with no trees, they began floating above the grass so they could travel faster. When they reached some woods again, they landed and again began walking through the woods. They repeated the walking and the floating a few times until they came to the edge of a particular woods.

EekaYor peaked out from the trees and looked at a brown house.

"A few years ago," EekaYor began. "I met someone at that house. I was on a team that went to different houses to see if the Christmas presents were showing up properly under the Christmas trees. If things were not working correctly, sometimes presents showed up outside in the snow or got stuck in the side of the house."

"I came to this house," EekaYor went on. "There was a little girl there who was about four years old at the time. The little girl spotted me. I did not run away. I froze in place. I don't know why, but I just started talking to her and getting to know her. She was the nicest child and she was so smart. I still visit her twice a year. I know the rules say that humans and Gift Givers should not be friends until Earth gets on the *Nice List*. But she is a good friend and she often gives me good ideas."

EekaYor and MacKack waited by the edge of the woods until dark. Through a second-floor window, they saw her parents putting her to bed. The parents then left her bedroom. EekaYor and MacKack made their move.

5 TASHA'S IDEA

EekaYor led the way to the house while MacKack stayed behind a few steps. The little girl, Tasha, was six years old now.

EekaYor started floating toward Tasha's second floor window. She looked like Peter Pan as she flew. She had a secret knock on the window that she always used with Tasha.

Tasha had not seen EekaYor in about six months. Tasha ran to the window and quickly opened it. EekaYor floated inside. Tasha hugged EekaYor's waist and pulled her down onto the floor. The two girls rolled around on the floor and giggled.

Quickly, they shushed each other to be quiet. They did not want her brother Marcus to wake up. He was in the next bedroom and he was about fourteen now.

Tasha loved the Peter Pan story. She had a Peter Pan outfit and one for Captain Hook. Tasha usually made EekaYor put on the Peter Pan outfit and fly around her bedroom. When EekaYor did that it made Tasha giggle so much.

When they were together, they always talked about how they first met.

At the age of three, Tasha stayed up all night long by the tree on Christmas Eve. Tasha did not see Santa Claus. She did see the Christmas presents beam under the tree. One minute, they were not there. The next minute they were there. Tasha told Mom and Dad the next morning. They did not believe her.

The next year Tasha was four years old. Again, she stayed up all night on Christmas Eve. She saw an elf come into the room where her Christmas tree was. The elf stopped in its tracks. Then, it came over and slowly sat down next to Tasha. They began to talk like they were old friends and introduced themselves to each other. Tasha felt close to EekaYor and trusted her. EekaYor told Tasha many things. She told Tasha things that humans did not know.

Tasha learned from EekaYor that Santa Claus was there to help people become nicer. She also learned that Santa Claus had been doing this for 250 years and people had not gotten much nicer. She also learned that people on other planets had become nicer much more quickly than humans did. It often took only twenty to forty years on other planets. People on Earth were hard to change.

Tasha learned that Earth was on the *Naughty List.* If Earth could get on the *Nice List,* then it would get many gifts from EekaYor's people. These gifts would help the planet Earth become cooler and cleaner.

After they were done retelling the story of how they first met, then they started catching up about the things that happened in the last six months.

Tasha showed EekaYor some of the things she was learning in school. She showed EekaYor her model of the solar system. It had eight planets made out of little balls of different colors. Tasha giggled. She knew that EekaYor had seen the real solar system with her own eyes. Tasha also knew that EekaYor was from another solar system from far away. EekaYor's solar system had fourteen planets.

EekaYor's face suddenly changed and she looked a bit sad.

"Tasha, I have some bad news," EekaYor began. "Earth only has a couple days left to get on the *Nice List.* The High Council is tired of waiting for humans to become nice."

EekaYor's head went down and she began to cry. Tasha put her arm around her and held her hand. This might be the last time that these two friends would ever see each other.

Just then, Tasha had an idea. "What if everyone across the Earth became happy at the same time? Would that get Earth on the *Nice List*?"

"Maybe," EekaYor said. "But how would you do that?"

Tasha said more, "The sadness I see in you, EekaYor, is the same sadness I see in my Mom and Dad. The bad things going on in the world make Mom and Dad very sad all the time. This sadness is everywhere."

Tasha went on after thinking, "I will ask Santa to take away my Christmas presents and give nice presents to my Mom and Dad. Maybe that would help."

Tasha stood up as her idea was growing bigger, "Maybe we can get all children in the world to do this. They will ask for presents for their parents and not get any for themselves."

Tasha now raised her hands above her head and looked up at the ceiling, "On Christmas morning, there will be so much joy and happiness in all the parents in the world. The children will show the world how to be nice—really nice."

"That sounds great!" EekaYor said. "But how are we going to do that?"

Just then, they heard a noise at the bedroom door. They did not have time to move before the door opened quickly. It was Marcus! He was tall and lanky and looked like he had just woken up. He saw that Tasha was not alone. There was a strange little person with her.

Marcus grabbed Captain Hook's plastic sword that was against the wall. With his other hand, he picked up Captain Hook's plastic hook off the floor. He was ready to fight EekaYor to protect Tasha.

"No, no," Tasha spoke up. "She's my friend! She's the one I told you about."

Marcus' jaw dropped open. His arms drooped. He dropped both the sword and the hook onto the floor.

Marcus then sat on the floor. He was puzzled and did not know what to think. Tasha had been telling him about her friend for two years, but he did not believe her. Her friend was real?

Marcus thought, "Tasha also told me how the Christmas presents appear under the tree like magic. Was that real, too?"

Marcus sat down on the floor and was quiet from his confusion.

"This is EekaYor," Tasha said to Marcus. "She is my friend."

"This is Marcus," Tasha said to EekaYor. "He is my brother."

Tasha updated Marcus about the sad things that she and EekaYor were discussing. Tasha then told her new idea to Marcus.

“How can we tell the children of the world to ask for presents for their parents?” Tasha asked.

“And not ask for any presents for themselves,” EekaYor added.

“Also, how can we keep this a secret from the parents?” Tasha asked. “We want it to be a surprise for them. This will add to their joy.”

“That’s easy,” Marcus said. “If I post a TikTok video of you, Tasha, telling this story, it will go viral.”

“I will post it on all my social media,” Marcus added. “Most parents don’t know what their kids are doing online. So, very few parents will see it. And parents won’t believe it, even if they do see it.”

“That’s a brilliant idea!” Tasha said.

“That is awesome,” EekaYor said as her face brightened a bit. “You two are awesome.”

EekaYor stood up and looked much happier.

“Okay, you’ve got work to do,” EekaYor added. “I’ve got work to do. Let’s get Earth on the *Nice List*.”

With that, they hugged goodbye. Tasha gave EekaYor a big hug. Marcus gave EekaYor kind of an awkward sideways hug.

EekaYor stepped onto the windowsill and floated outside to the lawn below. Tasha and Marcus then saw someone with a huge red beard down in the yard. It was MacKack. EekaYor and MacKack waved goodbye. Then, they floated to the woods towards their ship.

Marcus and Tasha made their plans to make the video the next day. It was late into the night on December 22. There were just two days until Christmas Eve.

6 MAKING PLANS

As EekaYor and MacKack floated back to their starship, they discussed their plans along the way.

"We don't know for sure that KisQualley and Mr. Hancock are working together," EekaYor said.

"But, things sure seem that way," MacKack responded.

"Maybe there is more data on Mr. Hancock's computer," EekaYor added.

"Or, maybe we can trick KisQualley into telling us," MacKack said.

"How would we do that?" EekaYor asked.

"Leave that to me," MacKack smiled.

They reached their ship and went inside.

"We will have to fly closer to your bio-computer so we can talk to it,"MacKack added.

They flew back to the woods west of New York City. This was the same place she parked her ship when she went to see Mr. Hancock. They now were close enough to talk to her bio-computer that was still inside Mr. Hancock's computer.

EekaYor told the bio-computer to look at all the data on Mr. Hancock's computer. At the same time, MacKack wrote a fake email from Mr. Hancock to KisQualley.

"How about something like this?" MacKack asked EekaYor.

'It was nice working with you,' MacKack typed. 'I wish you all the best when you return home to your own planet.'

"What do you think?" MacKack asked.

"It's pretty simple," EekaYor said. "You think it is enough to get KisQualley to admit something secret about Mr. Hancock? Everyone knows that KisQualley is going home after his time working with Earth. How about adding one more line?"

EekaYor reached over and typed one more line, 'Enjoy your riches.' EekaYor and MacKack thought that Mr. Hancock gave KisQualley rare metals from Earth. KisQualley's home planet does not have these metals. So, they would be worth a lot of money on his planet.

The email now read: "*It was nice working with you. I wish you all the best when you return home to your own planet. Enjoy your riches.*"

"That should get some response from KisQualley," MacKack agreed.

EekaYor sent the email to her bio-computer, which would then email it to KisQualley from Mr. Hancock's email account.

As they waited for a reply, they talked some more about Tasha's video.

"If Tasha's video goes around the world," MacKack began, "children will be saying that they don't want any presents. They will also say that they want Santa to give presents to their parents."

"The children will send so many emails and letters to Santa," EekaYor said. "All the emails will arrive a couple days before Christmas. Our computers at the North Pole will not be able to deal with so many emails in such a short amount of time."

"We are going to have to be there to keep the computers working," MacKack added. "The Gift Givers at the North Pole don't know that so many emails are coming."

"The Gift Givers at the North Pole will catch us," EekaYor said. "But, we have to go to the North Pole. We have to get the computers ready for all the new emails."

7 THE LOWEST POINT

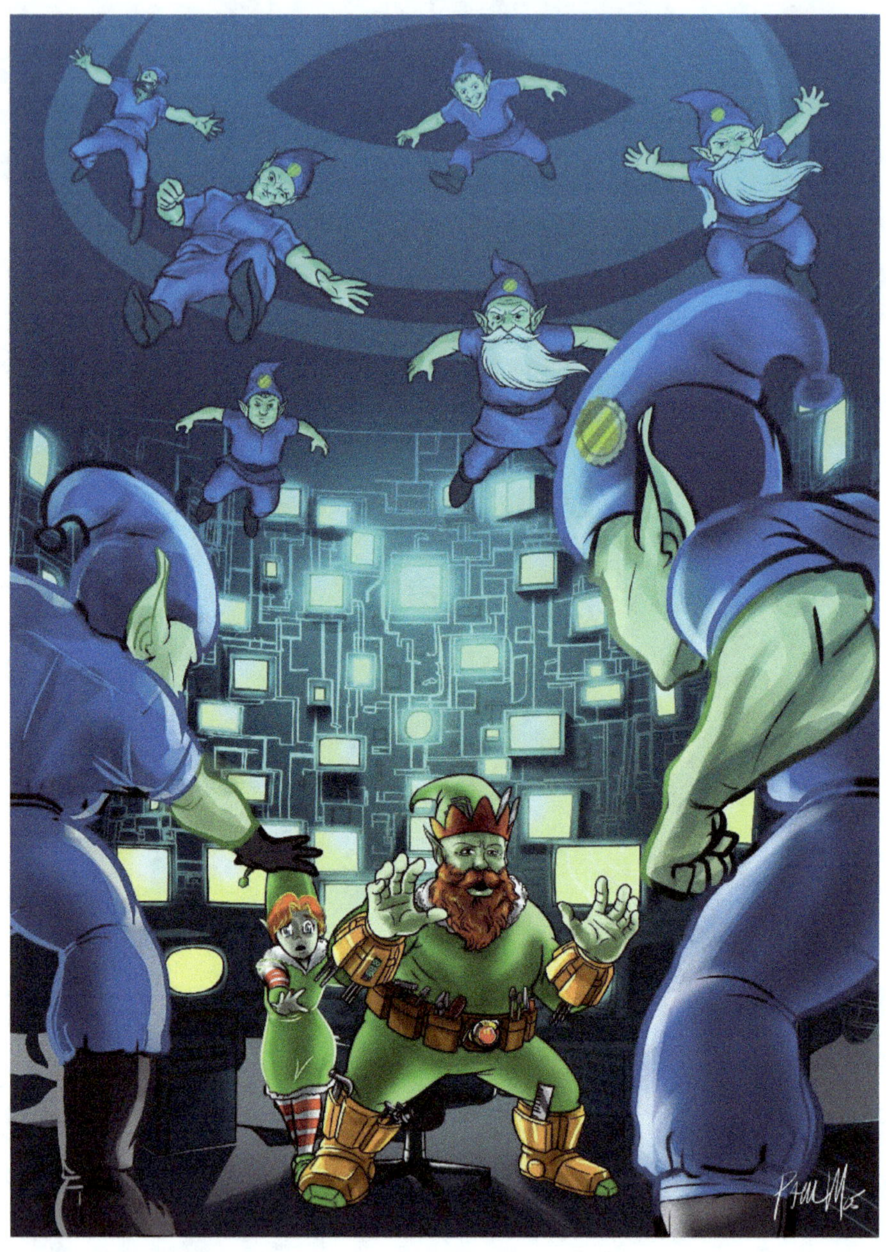

It was now the evening of December 23. EekaYor and MacKack were ready to go to the North Pole. Then, an alarm went off that KisQualley had emailed back in response to the fake email message.

Don't contact me this way. But make sure you're ready to load up my ship with the good stuff. Now, there is no hope of Earth getting on the Nice List. So, you can keep making a lot of money as people will always be fighting.

Mr. Hancock was giving KisQualley something for leaving Earth alone. That was all that EekaYor and MacKack needed to know. Mr. Hancock was crooked. That was no surprise. But KisQualley, the head of the Gift Givers, was also corrupt. That was a big surprise.

EekaYor and MacKack flew their ship to the North Pole. In the dark, they were able to sneak into the computer rooms with no one seeing them. They worked to make the computer memory bigger so it could hold all the emails that would come in.

After a while, the emails started arriving at the North Pole. Marcus had posted Tasha's video. It was spreading quickly. Many children and teens were watching it. It would soon become a viral video.

EekaYor and MacKack found Tasha's video online. She was so cute and her story was so interesting! Children sent their emails to Santa soon after they watched Tasha's video.

The emails started out as a few here and there. Soon, the number of emails grew into the millions. MacKack did the math and thought there would be a total of five billion emails before the night was over. Each email said about the same thing: "*Santa, please give my parents nice presents this Christmas. They deserve it. I don't want any presents for myself.*"

It was good that EekaYor and MacKack were both there. The computers would have crashed if they had not expanded the memory. They just had to stay there through the night to make sure the computers kept working. Things went very well for a while.

Then, without even a sound, the elf, PenNickel, got an alert that the computers were using a lot of power. He peeked into the computer room and saw EekaYor and MacKack. PenNickel called the guards.

The guards knew all the tricks that EekaYor and MacKack might try. They were ready for EekaYor and MacKack to try to cloak so they could not be seen. They were ready for them to try floating away. Some guards stayed on the floor and others floated in the air to make a half-sphere shape that surrounded them completely. In no time, the guards had them.

MacKack was known by every elf at the North Pole and EekaYor was somewhat famous. They knew that she was the youngest elf to be on the High Council. The guards were puzzled that these two great elves were going to be put in prison. But the guards followed KisQualley's orders and put them in prison.

EekaYor and MacKack were each put in their own prison cell. They could not see each other, nor could they speak to each other. It was early in the morning on December 24. Santa came by to talk to MacKack and EekaYor.

"I have to follow KisQualley's orders, too," Santa began. "But we'll get to the bottom of this. MacKack, you are my most trusted friend. EekaYor, everyone is so proud of you for being on the High Council at such a young age. There must be much more to the story. As you know, I am very busy today and tonight. I cannot listen to your stories now, but there will be time later."

To pass the time in his cell, MacKack sang Christmas carols in his deep, gravelly voice. EekaYor imagined the story of *Peter Pan* over and over again. It was going to be a long day and then a long Christmas Eve.

8 A BREAKTHROUGH

LIVE
LIVE

Christmas Eve went off without any problems. All the presents ended up in the right homes. No news reached EekaYor and MacKack. They had no idea if Tasha's idea was really working.

Very early on Christmas morning, the guards returned to the prison. KisQualley sent orders to bring the prisoners to the space station where he would judge them and sentence them to prison. EekaYor and MacKack were taken into a spaceship that flew quickly to the asteroid belt.

With handcuffs on, EekaYor and MacKack walked with the guards into the large stone room of the High Council. KisQualley was sitting there upon his big stone chair. He wore a long, multi-colored cape that partially covered a shiny robe. The High Council, except for EekaYor, were seated about the big stone table. The Council was also wearing their best outfits consisting of capes and robes. When the prisoners were in front of KisQualley, he stood up to show how big he was and how small they were.

"We are leaving Earth forever after today," KisQualley said. "Today, I will tell you how long you two will be in prison."

Just then, an alarm began to sound. It was a sound that no one had ever heard before. Even MacKack, who made the alarm, almost forgot what it sounded like.

It was the alarm that Earth was ready for the *Nice List*. After 250 years, it had come true! Tasha's idea worked!

News shows from Earth began to show on the walls of the High Council's room. Children did not ask for any toys. They asked for presents for their parents to show how much they appreciated their parents. The parents were so filled with joy that their children were so generous and thoughtful. The children felt a special joy inside that came from caring for other people. Social media was filled with happy posts. The joy spread through the whole world. The joy went on and on hour after hour.

KisQualley yelled loudly to try to regain order, "It is too late! We will leave Earth on the *Naughty List* forever."

"You are too late!" EekaYor yelled back at KisQualley.

"You belong in prison!" KisQualley yelled back.

"She does not!" spoke a friendly but loud voice. Everyone in the room turned to see who was coming into the room. It was Santa Claus. Everyone in the room stood out of respect.

"And I have proof that you belong in prison, KisQualley," Santa added. "Mr. Hancock's ship is loading KisQualley's ship right now with rare earth metals. That is against the law. Both Mr. Hancock and KisQualley wanted Earth to stay on the *Naughty List.* But the goodness of the children of Earth led by EekaYor and MacKack were able to get Earth on the *Nice List.*"

All the High Council members cheered. This is the day they had all been waiting for since they arrived at Earth many years ago. KisQualley almost made them forget what they had come to Earth to do. Guards freed EekaYor and MacKack from their handcuffs. They put the handcuffs on KisQualley and led him away.

9 FIRST CONTACT AND BEYOND

Later on Christmas Day, children and their parents around the world ran outside and stared up at the sky. Spaceships of all sizes landed near groups of humans. Elf-like beings came out from the ships to play with the children and greet the parents. The elves then invited families to come onboard to fly across the sky with them. Elves and humans celebrated together throughout the night and into the next day.

During the next day, elves started delivering the high-tech tools to engineers and scientists around the world. One type of machine created energy for free without making any pollution. Another type of huge machine made the air pure. Still another machine cleaned the water. Thousands of these machines were installed around the world. Further, millions of little flying machines were released high into the atmosphere where they would absorb some of the heat from the sun so that the planet was a bit cooler.

The elves showed the scientists how their ships were able to travel so quickly through space. Humans would soon be traveling to other planets and solar systems.

All wars stopped because most wars are caused by people fighting over resources of some kind: land, energy, water, food, among other things. With the new machines from the elves, there were enough resources for everyone. People did not have to fight over them. Why fight over energy when energy could be made for free? Why fight over land when soon your people could travel to other planets to live? Many of the reasons for fighting disappeared.

About the only human who was angry about all these changes was Mr. Hancock. Without fighting, he would not be able to sell his weapons and make money that way.

Most of the elves packed up to return to their home planet. Some would retire and stay there. Others would vacation at home and then get ready for another mission to help another planet get on the *Nice List*. Still others stayed on Earth to continue to help the humans with the new technology and help guard against any new wars breaking out.

EekaYor decided to stay on Earth to be close to her best friend Tasha. EekaYor was part of the team that would help make sure that humans would not go back to their old ways of fighting and making the Earth dirty and hot.

MacKack decided to return to his home planet to retire and continue to invent things. Santa Claus stayed on Earth and continued to bring joy to children every year.

The elves learned an important lesson from Earth. When working with other planets, get the children involved from the start. The children can lead the way to make real change. In this way, planets would get on the *Nice List* much more quickly.

Humans changed drastically that Christmas. They got on the *Nice List*. They made *First Contact* with aliens. They jumped ahead in technology in a way that did away with most reasons for war. They could suddenly travel to far planets and solar systems. Their dreams expanded from small dreams about the Earth to large dreams involving the entire galaxy.

For a while, it looked like this Christmas was going to be the last Christmas, but it became the first Christmas of a new era of humanity.

The End

GLOSSARY

Asteroid

A large rock that flies through outer space. The large rock is smaller than a planet. It is often a chunk of rock, so it is not round and smooth.

Asteroid belt

When many asteroids fly together around the sun, the group is called an asteroid belt. There is an asteroid belt between the planets Mars and Jupiter.

Beaming

A thing suddenly appears in a place. Really, it started in one place and was "beamed" to another place.

Beings

Anything that is alive can be called a *being*. Humans are beings and can be called *human beings*.

Billionaire

A person who has a billion dollars, which is $1,000,000,000.

Bio-computer

People are working on making biological things into computers. Cells make up people, animals, and plants. When one cell or a group of cells acts like a computer, it is called a bio-computer.

Brilliant

Something great, such as a *brilliant idea*.

Captain Sideways

This superhero solves problems for people in an odd or uncommon way.

Cells

People, animals, and plants are all made up of cells. In a human or an animal, cells can be of different kinds. There are skin cells, blood cells, bone cells, and many other kinds of cells.

Clean Energy

When energy does not make nature dirty, then it is called *clean energy*. For example, a windmill makes energy without making nature dirty. Cars that use gasoline make nature around it dirty, so gasoline cars do not use clean energy.

Cloaking

A thing can be made so that no one can see it. Light bends around the thing so that it looks like the thing is not there.

Computer memory

The part of a computer that stores the data. In this way, it remembers it.

Council

A group of people that gather to discuss things and make decisions.

Energy

Energy allows machines to work and beings to think and move.

Extraterrestial

This word means that someone or something is not from Earth.

Geeky

A person who likes math and science can be said to be *geeky*.

Gravity

A force that keeps things close together. A rock falls to the ground because of gravity. A planet stays in orbit around a star because of gravity.

Handcuff

Two metal rings that connect by a short chain. One ring goes around one wrist. The other wring goes around the other wrist. Police often use handcuffs so a person cannot easily use their hands.

High Council

The group of people that has the final say. Their decisions are final. No other group of people can change the decisions of the *High Council*.

High-Tech

This term means technology that is very complex.

Invention

An object that someone made to do something. For example, a pen is an invention that is used to write. A shoe is an invention that you wear on your feet when you walk.

Million

A number with six zeroes behind it. So, one million is 1,000,000 and two million is 2,000,000.

Quantum mechanics

A way of explaining how the smallest parts of the world work. These smallest parts sometimes act in a strange manner. For example, at the smallest levels, things can be many things at the same time. When someone looks at them, they become just one thing. So, the person only sees one thing, but just a moment ago, the one thing was many different things all at the same time.

Sideways

To move toward something from the side, not from the front or back. Also, to solve a problem in an odd or uncommon way.

Skylight

A window on a ceiling that lets light into the room.

Social media

Online apps such as *Facebook* and *TikTok* that allow people to connect and share online.

Spaceship

A ship that flies through outer space.

Space Station

A large place in outer space that is built by humans or other beings. People can live and work there. Spaceships can travel there.

Starship

A ship that can fly in outer space. It can fly between the planets. Some can fly between the stars.

Superhero

A good being that uses their great powers to do good things.

Tech

The word “tech” is short for technology.

Technology

Machines that do things that people need done.

Trillionaire

A person who has a trillion dollars, which is $1,000,000,000,000.

Viral

If a person puts up something on social media and many people see it, then it has gone viral.

DISCUSSION GUIDE
FOR SMALL GROUPS, CLASSES, AND INDIVIDUAL REFLECTION

1. Why is Earth on the *Naughty List*? What do humans do that is wrong and hurtful to others and to the planet?

2. Do all humans do bad and harmful things or are there just a few very powerful people who cause most of the problems on Earth? Explain your answer.

3. Imagine another species on another planet that only took thirty years to get on the *Nice List.* What was this species like when the elves first arrived compared to humans?

4. Is it possible that there is a species on a planet that was on the *Nice List* from the beginning? Why or why not?

5. Were the elves ever on the *Naughty List?* Why or why not?

6. The leader of the elves, KisQualley, seems to be very mean. How can a group of generous elves have such a mean, selfish leader?

7. Mr. Hancock is still on Earth. Is he now very nice or will he try to do harmful, selfish things again?

8. MacKack created some incredible inventions:

    a. how presents get beamed under the Christmas trees
    b. how a wrapped present becomes what the child wants when the present is opened, and
    c. how the alarm system works that detects when humans are ready to be on the *Nice List*.

    Which of MacKack's inventions is his greatest invention? Why?

9. EekaYor is a young inventor and has already invented a bio-computer that is so small that it is about the size of a single cell in the body. What could be other great inventions that she could create in the future?

10. The elves hide their space station in a large asteroid and they hide some of their ships inside small asteroids that are traveling in Earth's direction. What are other things they could use the asteroids for that the story does not mention?

11. In chapter 5 of the story, we learn that the solar system that EekaYor is from has fourteen planets while Tasha's solar system has only eight planets. Imagine and describe how EekaYor's solar system and planet differ from our solar system and planet.

12. In chapter 5, Tasha understands the sad news that EekaYor has told her even though Tasha's parents have never talked to Tasha about it. Would you rather have your parents and friends tell you sad news or keep it a secret from you? Why?

13. Do you agree or disagree with the following passage from chapter 9 about getting help from the children? Why or why not?

The elves learned an important lesson from Earth. When working with other planets, get the children involved from the start. The children can lead the way to make real change. In this way, planets would get on the Nice List much more quickly.

14. Do you agree or disagree with the following passage about war from chapter 9? Why or why not?

All wars stopped because most wars are caused by people fighting over resources of some kind: land, energy, water, food, among other things. With the new machines from the elves, there were enough resources for everyone. People did not have to fight over them. Why fight over energy when energy could be made for free? Why fight over land when soon your people could travel to other planets to live? Many of the reasons for fighting disappeared.

15. *EekaYor decided to stay on Earth to be close to her best friend Tasha* (from chapter 9). Imagine and describe what EekaYor's next adventure might look like.

ABOUT THE AUTHORS

Tony McCaffrey

is a computer science teacher and a researcher in creativity and problem solving. He loves science fiction and Christmas, so combined them into a story. He created this story during the COVID-19 pandemic because he needed a story of hope himself and hopes that it gives others hope, too.

Dave Goulet

is an author and screenwriter living in Toronto. He spent many of his formative years as a volunteer in the South Pacific learning how to paddle outrigger canoes. He has been "navigating the stars" ever since, especially those that shine brightest at Christmas.

Previous Books

Goulet, D. (2023). *Black and Blue Horizons.* Batini Books.

Goulet, D. (2021). *Halos Rising: A Book on Fantastic Future Saints*. Novalis.

McCaffrey, T. (2020). *Hooray for a Different Way.* Eagle Hill Publishing.

McCaffrey, T. (2019). *Infinite Learning Diversity: Uncovering the Hidden Talents Of Our Students.* Rowman & Littlefield.

McCaffrey, T. (2018). *Overcome Any Obstacle to Creativity.* Rowman & Littlefield.

McCaffrey, A.J. (2006). *Fractalia: Episode 1: Reversing the Tipping Point*. Booklocker.

McCaffrey, A.J. (2002). *Emmanuel McClue and the Mystery of the Shroud.* Ambassador Books.

McCaffrey, A.J. (2002). *Emmanuel's Manual: A Teacher's Resource for Emmanuel McClue and the Mystery of the Shroud.* Ambassador Books.

Goulet, D. (2000). *Looney Tombs: Confessions of a Small Town Funeral Director's Son.* General Store Publishing House.

McCaffrey, T. (1997). *My Bedtime Prayer*. Loyola Press, Chicago.

McCaffrey, T. (1996). *Storytellers of God: Teacher's Toolbox.* Sheed & Ward.

ABOUT THE ILLUSTRATOR

Paul Ritz Magtrayo is a freelance graphic artist and illustrator based in Marikina, Manila, Philippines. His passion is drawing, especially *Marvel*- and *DC*-like heroes. He is passionate about creating diverse concepts across various forms of art. In every piece he produces, he invests his full effort, dedication, and attention to detail. To him and his family, each creation is a true masterpiece. Whether abstract or realistic, on any medium—traditional or digital—he is capable of bringing ideas to life. While he may be new to the professional art industry, his potential is undeniable; with continued learning and refinement of his skills, he is poised to become a remarkable force in the art world. Born with an innate talent for artistry, Paul is determined to leave a lasting legacy, transforming the landscape of art in ways the world has yet to witness. When he is not drawing, he enjoys playing badminton and volleyball. He comes from a large family of seven, where he is the only son among many daughters.

🌿 "How to Leave a Review" Guide for Readers

✅ How to Leave a Review for a ShelteringTree.Earth Book

Thank you for supporting our authors. Reviews help readers discover books that speak to their hearts and spirits. Even a short review makes a meaningful difference.

Here's a simple guide to help you leave a review on Amazon, Goodreads, ShelteringTreeMedia, or any other book review site.

✅ 1. What to Write in a Review

Your review does *not* need to be long or complicated.

A few sentences is enough.

You can share:

- what you enjoyed
- what you learned
- how the book made you feel
- who you think would benefit from it
- your favorite part or takeaway

You do **not** need to summarize the entire book.

✅ 2. How to Leave a Review on Amazon

Step 1: Go to the book's Amazon page

Search for the title or use the link provided by the author.

Step 2: Scroll down to "Customer Reviews"

Click **"Write a customer review."**

Step 3: Choose a star rating

5 stars = excellent

1 star = poor

Step 4: Write your review

A few sentences is perfect.

Step 5: Click Submit

That's it — your review is live.

✅ 3. How to Leave a Review on Goodreads

Step 1: Log in to Goodreads

(You can create a free account if you don't have one.)

Step 2: Search for the book

Click on the correct edition.

Step 3: Click the stars to rate the book

This alone counts as a review.

Step 4: Click "Write a Review"

Add your thoughts and click **Save**.

✅ 4. How to Leave a Review on ShelteringTreeMedia.com

Step 1: Go to the ARC tab on ShelteringTreeMedia.com

Step 2: Scroll down to the Review box

Step 3: Fill in the form

Step 4: Click SUBMIT

ARC Team members will be sent a coupon once the review is posted under the book in our shop page.

✅ 4. Tips for Helpful Reviews

- Be honest
- Be kind
- Be specific
- Keep spoilers minimal
- Share how the book impacted you

✅ 5. Why Reviews Matter

Reviews help:

- authors reach new readers
- bookstores and libraries decide what to carry
- online algorithms recommend the book
- readers discover books that nourish their spirit

Your voice truly makes a difference.

SHELTERING
TREE
Earth
Publishing
ShelteringTreeMedia.com

www.ingramcontent.com/pod-product-compliance
Lightning Source LLC
LaVergne TN
LVHW010618110826
845149LV00003B/962

* 9 7 8 1 9 6 3 2 7 2 1 2 3 *